Praise for

"Having lived in Ho
yoga professionally I new age
community. I had heard many good things about the psychic reader Anne Hassett, also known as Acushla, but it wasn't until 2017 that I actually got to meet her. The biggest impression she made on me was her common sense, thoughtful and mature attitude—something I hadn't expected from an angel whisperer. Her good sense of humor and bright outlook were contagious. She seems to have a foot in each of two worlds, spiritual and material, which makes her tried and true perspectives worth hearing. All this shines in her book *Dynamic Ageless You*. Reading it is like spending time with a real wise woman. Highly recommended."

—Sravaniya DiPecoraro, ACBSP,
Astrological and psychic consultant, Founder and Director of Barefoot Philosopher Press, and author of *Basic Bhagavad Gita*

"As a doctor and scientist I would agree with everything in this book. We can not only change our day to day reality but also actually affect our own aging process. These concepts are based in truth and totally empowering."

—Dr. Susan Jamieson, MB ChB, MRCGP,
and author of *Medical to Mystical*

DYNAMIC AGELESS YOU

DYNAMIC AGELESS YOU

Belief shapes Biology
So ...
GIVE YOURSELF
A FAITH-LIFT

by Anne M. Hassett

Acushla's Angels

Second edition 2019

Images courtesy of Unsplash. www.unsplash.com
The following images appear in the public domain: Albert Einstein, pages 54-55.

Library of Congress Cataloging-in-Publication Data
Hassett, Anne
Dynamic Ageless You

1. Neuropsychology 2. Ageing 3. Healthy Living

ISBN: 978-1-9161807-3-4 (paperback)
ISBN: 978-1-9161807-1-0 (ePub)
ISBN: 978-1-9161807-2-7 (Kindle)

www.AcushlasAngels.com

Contents

DYNA

MIC

To-Do List .... or should I say, 'To BE' list!

AGE

LESS

Y

U

Foreword

At my age of 82, friends and clients constantly remark on how young, fit and vital I am. They don't believe me when I tell them my age. They ask what is my secret.

I suppose my secret is that I never think of age. I'm not even good at guessing other peoples ages. I see the whole person, their energy and their attitude.

I do not believe that the number of years that have elapsed since I was born actually preclude me from very much. I just don't think like that.

Within reason, I still believe that I can do most things. Maybe I can't swim the English channel or climb Everest or run a marathon. I know people of my age who do run marathons, but all that huffing and puffing, panting and sweating does not turn me on!

We can keep our bodies fluid and mobile in much gentler ways. I love to dance. You can join a dance class or you can just dance around your own kitchen. And it can be great fun.

I am convinced that the 'Big Secret' is attitude and belief. Both attitudes and beliefs can be changed. To make this change takes persistence and effort to begin with, but it soon becomes a habit.

The information it contains can help you to stay younger and fitter and happier for longer.

If you wish to read further and do further research of your own, then please go on to read the wonderful books I am recommending to you. These books are full of facts and valuable information and make exciting reading, especially if they can whet your appetite to learn more about staying younger, healthier and fitter for longer. You can do it.

Dynamic
Ageless
You

Combining Ancient Wisdom and Modern Science, we now have the understanding, the information and the tools to live longer, fully functional lives.

Science today, is what miracles were to our ancestors.

A shift in our beliefs can extend our life span and revolutionise our ideas about ageing. The belief in growing old and ageing is one of the biggest limiting factors in our lives.

Up to about the age of twenty-five, we are told that we are 'too young' ... 'too young' to know very much, 'too young' to have any experience or wisdom, 'too young' to be considered for many jobs and positions in our society.

Then, very quickly it seems, we get to forty and now we are 'too old' ... too old to do the job

properly, or so they would tell us, too old to attract Mr. or Miss Right.

Too old: past it!

That gives us a mere fifteen years in which to be a useful member of today's society.

What a waste and how ridiculous!

Does it have to be that way? Certainly not. Do we have to age? Certainly not. Of course we grow older, but we do not have to age in the traditional way.

“Things do not change; we change.”

Henry David Thoreau.

Can you change the ageing process?

Our bodies are made up of zillions of cells. Those cells are constantly renewing themselves.

I have always wondered, if our cells are constantly dying off and constantly renewing themselves, why would they renew themselves with old worn out cells?

Our bodies have intelligence, I thought. So why would our bodies do something as stupid as replace dying cells with cells that were less than perfect?

Its because we tell them to. We do not consciously tell them to, but in our thinking patterns and our individual and collective beliefs we are sending our cells that message all the time.

We are so used to sending out that message that it has become automatic and we do not consciously think about it anymore.

We are like those who once believed that the earth was flat. It was perfectly obvious to them, all they had to do was look

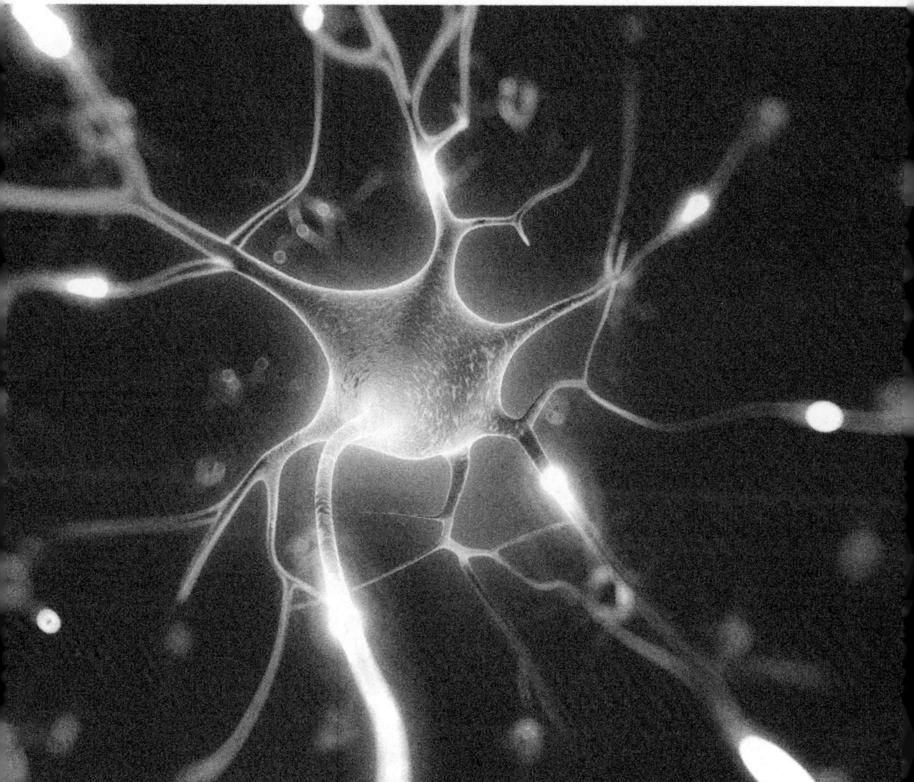

Neurons (also called neurones or nerve cells) are the fundamental units of the brain and nervous system, the cells responsible for receiving sensory input from the external world, for sending motor commands to our muscles, and for transforming and relaying the electrical signals at every step in between.

around them. Their eyes and vision told them that they were standing on flat ground. They had no way of knowing that the earth was round. They would (and did) think that anyone who thought that the earth was anything other than flat was barking mad.

We have fallen into the pattern of thinking that because we are getting older in years, we must also suffer from the deterioration of ageing and anyone who suggests otherwise must be barking mad!

Through erroneous beliefs about many things, we have fouled up our belief systems to such an extent that we have lost touch with the truth of who we are and what we are truly capable of. We are collectively hypnotised by cultural beliefs which do not serve us well.

When we know the truth and know who and what we are, we can change those old erroneous beliefs and set ourselves free. Free to live longer, healthier and more productive lives.

Many of us have belonged to metaphysical or spiritual groups. We have worked with positive thinking and done our affirmations. We know that we create our own reality and that there is a power in the universe which can heal.

Yet, we don't really believe it: not deep down.

The majority of us are operating from knee-jerk conditioning and are still operating from the same paradigm as our ancestors. We think or assume that the thoughts we are thinking are our own, but, in fact, we are downloading them from the entrenched beliefs of the collective consciousness.

We need to stop and really question what we are thinking and rewrite the paradigm.

Neuroscientists tell us that 95% of our thoughts are actually coming from our subconscious mind, which is not aware and is conditioned and pre-programmed by what has been fed into it by the race mind.

You can read all the positive thinking books, attend all the metaphysical courses and classes, but if you do not have a deep down commitment to change and a deep desire to change, nothing much is going to happen, and the biggest change has to take place in your beliefs.

Watch your wandering thoughts; master them. Then you become your own master.

It is also important to know deep down that, despite all appearances to the contrary, the universe is on your side.

Age is a construct of the mind. Getting old is a belief. Changing our beliefs, we change our biology.

"There are two ways to be fooled. One is to believe what isn't true: the other is to refuse to believe what is true."

Soren Kirkegaard,
Danish Philosopher.

The Field

We live in a field of energy: The 'stuff' of which our reality is comprised.

The space around us is not empty; it is made up of Quantum energy.

Just as waves of sound rippling through sand or water will create patterns in the sand or water, our thoughts ripple through the fabric of The Field to create our reality.

Our thoughts, which create our beliefs, have therefore an incredible power to mould and shape the 'stuff' which comprises the malleable field. This field can be understood as a matrix or a hologram.

It is a field shared by everything and everyone. Nothing and no one is separate from anything else.

Just as an observer in an experiment will influence the

experiment, we influence the field around us. Science has discovered that human DNA actually affects the field in ways that seem to defy logic.

Just as DNA affects the field, our thoughts and beliefs affect our DNA.

So, since our beliefs affect our DNA and our DNA affects the field. Our beliefs hold the key to our power to change our biology.

To change our world, we must focus not on what we see, but on what we want to see.

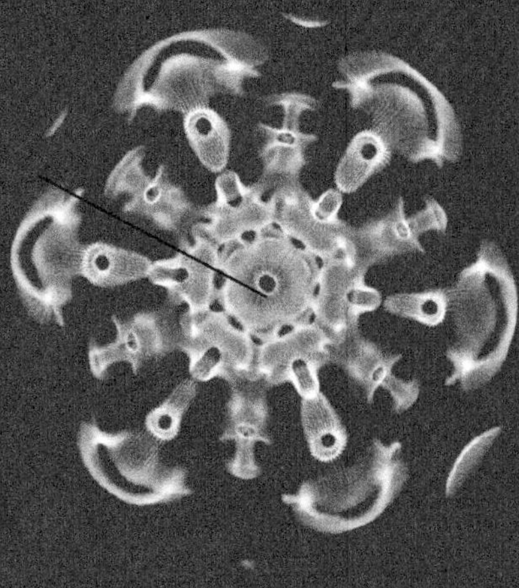

Cymatics is based on the principle that when sound encounters a membrane such as your skin or the surface of water (shown here,) it imprints an invisible pattern of energy. In other words, the periodic vibrations in the sound sample are converted and become periodic water ripples, creating beautiful geometric patterns that reveal the once hidden realm of sound.

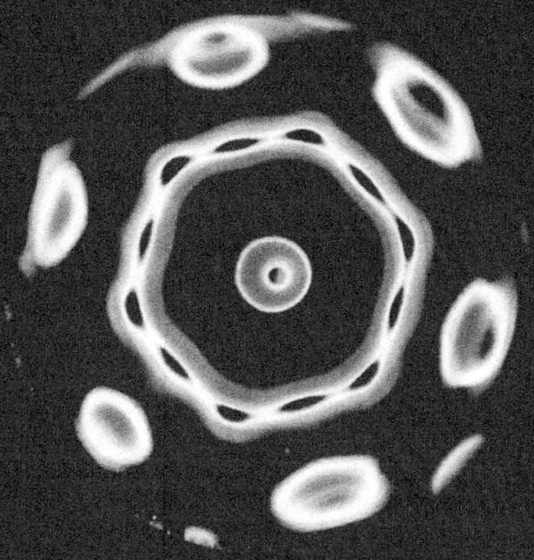

Cymatics is the name coined by Hans Jenny (1904-1972), a Swiss physician and natural scientist, to describe visible sound. Considered the father of cymatics, he laid important foundations for this emergent science. Jeff Volk of Macromedia Publishing has single-handedly championed Hans Jenny and republished Jenny's 1970's book "Cymatics: A Study of Wave Phenomena."

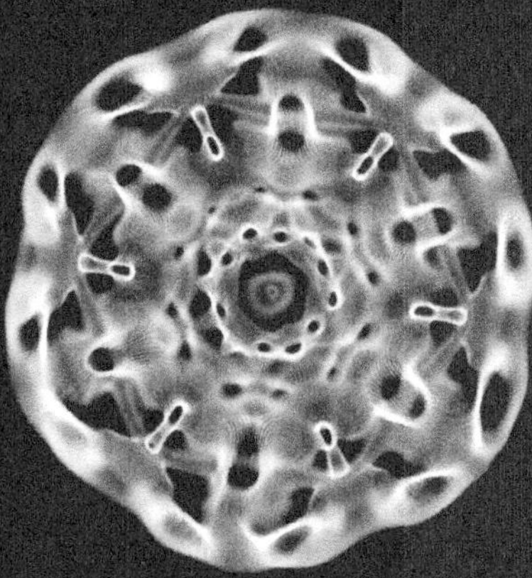

Sound lies at the heart of every aspect of Nature, underpinning all of Creation. The new science of visual sound—cymatics—will, in the future, enable humanity to understand far more about our world and Universe than we ever could with conventional instrumentation. The effect that sound can have on water and since our body is comprised mainly of water it is clear that the sound environment is important to our health.

"The moment you change your perception, is the moment you rewrite the chemistry of your body."

Dr. Bruce Lipton Ph.D.,
Cell Biologist and Research Scientist.

What are we?

The old Newtonian scientific paradigm known as Classical Physics saw our bodies as mindless machines. Our medical systems until very recently used this premise to treat disease. In the past eighty years Quantum Physics has come to the fore and a whole new understanding of reality has emerged.

Q: How much of an atom is empty space?

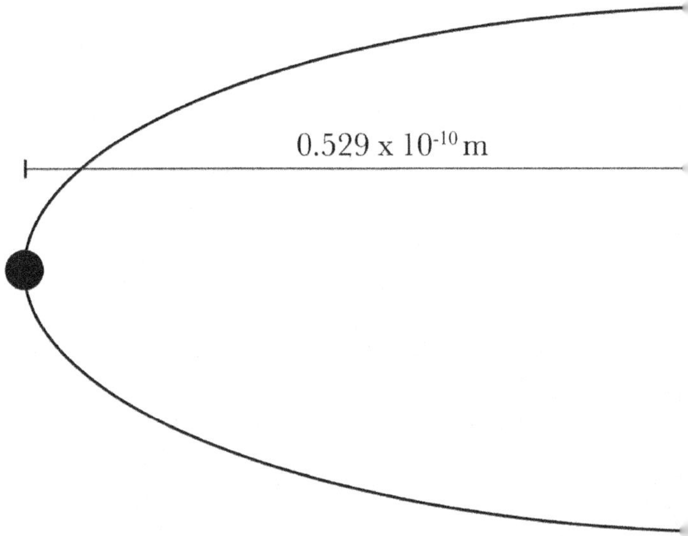

Let's take a look at an atom of hydrogen to see how empty it really is. Of course, this diagram isn't drawn to scale...

A hydrogen atom is made from a single proton that's circled by a single electron. How big is a hydrogen atom? The radius of a hydrogen atom is known as the Bohr Radius, which is equal to 0.529×10^{-10} meters. That means that a hydrogen atom has a volume of about 6.2×10^{-31} cubic meters.

How big is the proton at the center of a hydrogen atom? Recent studies indicate that protons have a radius of about 0.84×10^{-15} meters, giving them a volume of about 2.5×10^{-45} cubic meters.

We need to do a little more math to find out how much of a hydrogen atom is empty space.

A: Very nearly all of it!

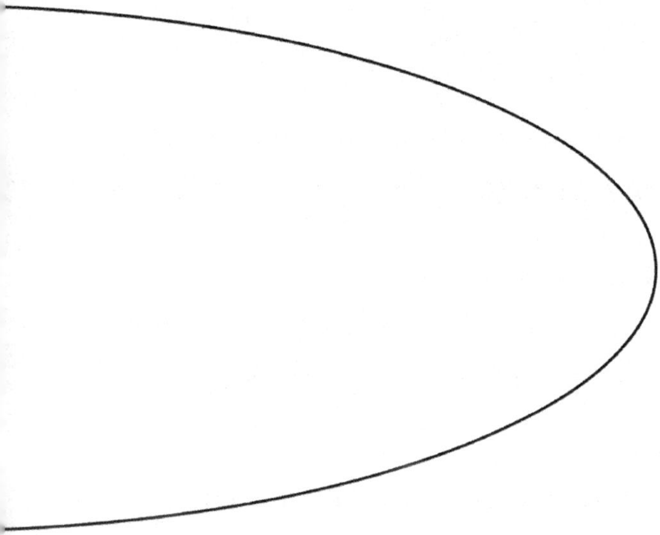

Percent Full = 100 × (Volume Filled / Total Volume)
Percent Full = 100 × (2.5×10^{-45} m^3 / 6.2×10^{-31} m^3)
Percent Full = 100 × (4×10^{-15})
Percent Full = 4×10^{-13} %
Percent Full = 0.0000000000004%

If 0.0000000000004% of a hydrogen atom is full, then the rest of it must be empty:

Percent Empty = 100% - Percent Full
Percent Empty = 100% - 0.0000000000004%
Percent Empty = 99.9999999999996%

The weight of scientific evidence is toppling the old paradigm.

In their true state our bodies are not solid matter but are composed of energy and information.

Our cells are made up of molecules and each molecule is comprised of atoms. Quantum physics tells us that every atom is more than 99.9999% empty space. Look at that figure again. 99.9999 percent empty space! And in this space are bundles of abstract vibrating energy.

Mind boggling!

So everything in the universe is swirling, vibrating energy. Non-stuff but very intelligent non-stuff.

So reality is, in fact, pulsing, vibrating intelligence. We are part of that unified field of energy. We are packets of intelligence and information.

We are Mind encoded and enshrouded in physical form. Intelligence hides and cloaks itself in the mask of matter.

We are bundles of information and beliefs.

In the law of psychosomatics, the body follows the instructions of the mind. So, as we change our mind and our beliefs, we change our bodies.

“Reality is merely an illusion, albeit a very persistent one.”

Albert Einstein.

The
Greater
You

There is a power within each one of us, the power that grows our hair and nails, beats our heart, changes our cells and performs the millions of tasks that we take for granted and which keep us alive rather that dead, and all without our conscious direction or interference.

spirit ... soul ...

... consciousness

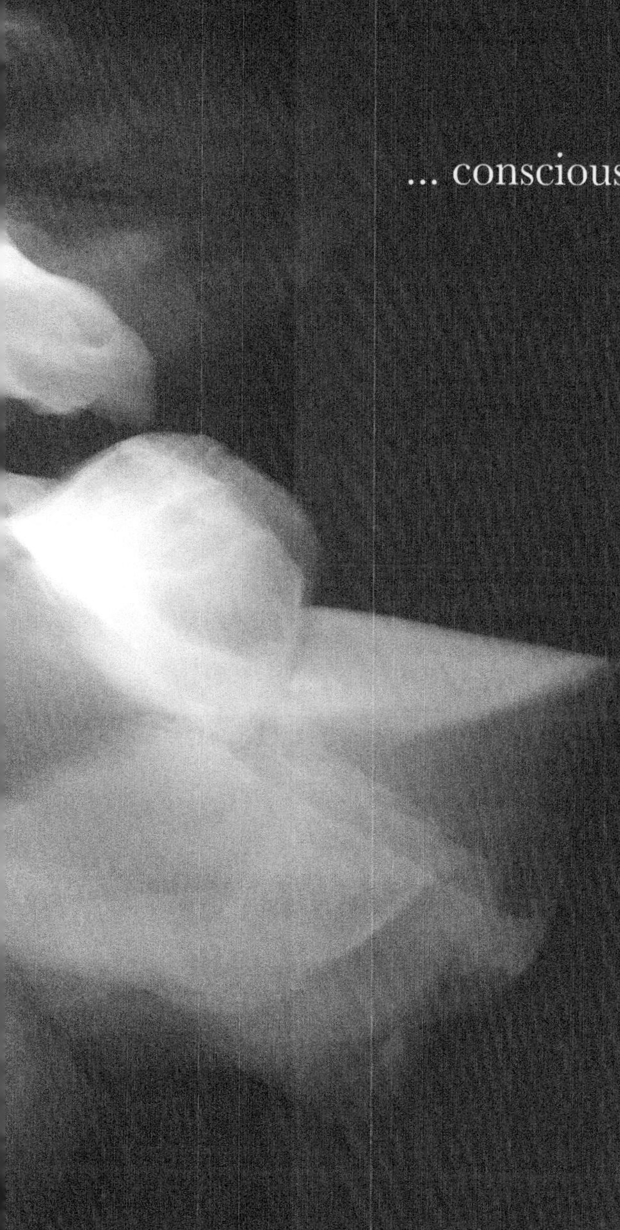

When that power leaves our body at the time of our death, then as physical entities, we truly are dead and we begin to decay. While we are alive that power is mighty. It is hugely intelligent and is responsive to our beliefs and to our will.

Whatever we may call that power .... soul, spirit, consciousness, it really doesn't matter what we call it, we all know we have it. Even those scientists who see us as pure machines cannot ignore it. Some of those scientists have referred to it as 'the ghost in the machine' but, it is there!

Whatever it is, it can be contacted, communicated with and commanded.

Our thoughts and beliefs are the commands we give to this power. As we change our thoughts and beliefs, we change the commands.

Many of our commands are unconscious and consequently can be destructive. When we say things like, "I'm too old for this", or "Old age never comes alone", or "At my age, I haven't got the energy". What kind of commands are we giving this almighty power? That is why it behoves us to be vigilant in the thoughts we entertain in our heads and the feelings we nurture in our hearts.

The number one step in changing ourselves is Awareness.

Our beliefs are extremely powerful. What we believe in our hearts will inevitably be out-pictured in our lives.

Why? Because, by our thoughts and beliefs, we have impressed upon the malleable substance of the field the thing or condition we are commanding into existence.

"We are the mirror and the face in the mirror."

Rumi. Mystical poet.

Vibes

We are bundles of pure energy. All energy is vibrating. These vibrations are on many frequencies. As we raise our vibrations we raise our frequencies. The opposite is also true.

Dr. David Hawkins has done extensive study calibrating different levels of consciousness. It would seem that at the higher levels of consciousness, such conditions as poverty, sickness, decay etc., cannot exist; they will not be a vibrational match to the higher frequencies.

So, as we raise our consciousness, we move away from unpleasant conditions. We need to leave behind such low vibrational frequencies as guilt, shame, anger, fear etc and give our time and attention to love, joy, trust, and vitality.

On the higher frequencies, we will have a vibrational match

with everything which is also on a high frequency. We become high vibrational attractors.

Health, youth and vigour are all on a high vibration. This is another reason to keep our vibrations as high as possible.

"It's the vibes man", the hippies used to say. They were right.

The power which resides within us is in a constant state of joy, but our minds choose to snack on dietary morsels of fear or guilt or uncertainty. This diet does us no good at all. We always have a choice.

To stay young and healthy, we need to choose a diet of positive

Levels of Consciousness

Enlightenment	
Peace	
Joy	
Love	POWER ↑
Reason	POWER ↑
Acceptance	POWER ↑
Willingness	POWER ↑
Neutrality	POWER ↑
Courage	POWER ↑
Pride	FORCE ↓
Anger	FORCE ↓
Desire	FORCE ↓
Fear	FORCE ↓
Grief	FORCE ↓
Apathy	FORCE ↓
Guilt	
Shame	

Consciousness Level

by Dr. David Hawkins

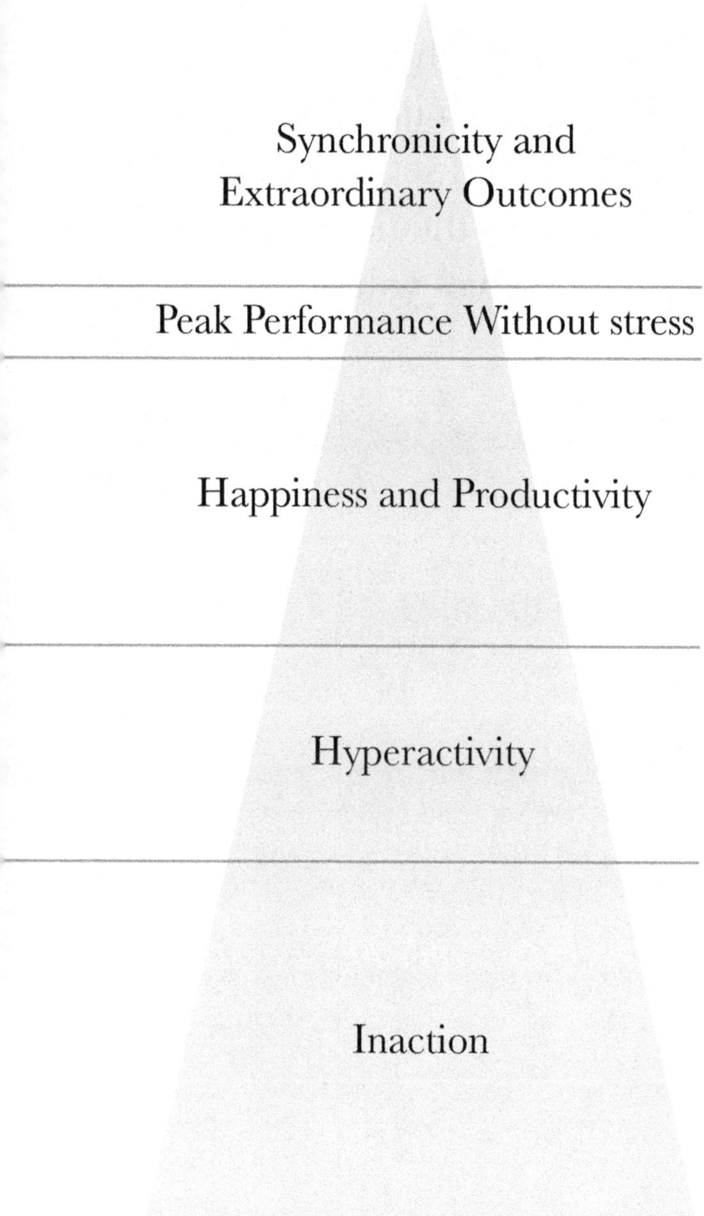

What We Experience

thoughts, which lead to positive feelings, which in turn affects our DNA and sets up a new paradigm in the field. We can think ourselves young.

"As a man thinks, so he is."

Jesus.

Beliefs

Ancient wisdom and modern science tell us that belief is what actually creates our experience. And belief is the intention we put out there to impress upon the 'stuff' that the universe is made of—to create our very reality. This 'stuff' is The Field.

We must have absolute faith in the power of belief for it to have power in our lives.

You may ask "How can our beliefs affect physical matter?"

Quantum physics tells us that the field is the primary substance and controlling force of the physical universe. The field is the 'stuff' that forms reality.

Because our thoughts, emotions, subtle energies and consciousness are invisible, they have been dismissed by classical physics: the old Newtonian paradigm. Consequently, we have not been in the habit of using them in our favour.

A hundred years ago, nobody would have believed that a T.V programme could pass through walls, glass and steel to get to a T.V set in our living room and all without wires in between. No wires, just waves.

Our thoughts are also waves, and very powerful ones too. Einstein said that matter is formed out of energy. Thought is energy. Our thought waves are far more powerful than we think. Once we accept how powerful our thoughts are, and take responsibility for them, we can use them to our advantage.

I read somewhere about a case of Multiple Personality

…f Σ …
Ruhe bef…

$$E = \frac{Mc^2}{\sqrt{1 - \frac{v^2}{c^2}}}$$

für den Z…
…h …f …

Disorder, where one of the personalities in the individual suffered from diabetes, yet when she was acting out her other personality, she did not have diabetes at all. Same body, different personality!

Surely it was the beliefs that were the influence.

"Every human being is the author of his own health or disease."

Buddha.

Three kinds of Ages

Since nobody is born with a clicker planted in their chest or arm that tells us how old they are, we have several different perspectives on how to classify someone's age.

1. Chronological Age. This is the age or number we find on our birth certificate, our driving licence and our passport. It is a record of the date on which we were born. It is just a number. Do not endow it with powers it does not need to have!

2. Biological Age. Our biological age reflects and describes the state of fitness of our organs and biological functions. This is where we can make significant differences.

3. Psychological Age. Reflects how old we think we are and how old we behave. I remember many years ago hearing a question being asked of

someone on a radio interview. The question was "How old would you think you were if you didn't know how old you were?" It gave me food for thought.

Only the first of these three 'ages' is an absolute unchangeable fact, but remember its only a number.

A 40 year old may be old and past it because his beliefs, his thoughts and his lifestyle tell him so, or you can have an 80 year old who is still buzzing about, being happy and enjoying life.

Before 1900, only one out of every ten people reached the age of 65. Today over 80% of

20
30

the population lives to over 65. We take better care of ourselves and we are more educated about how to look after ourselves, but we also see others living longer, so we know that it can be done.

Research has shown that death is rarely from wear and tear, it is usually as a result of some disease. Our mind-set can trigger disease, look at the word ... dis-ease: it means not being at ease. Wear and tear aside, our bodies actually benefit from use.The more we use our bodies, the better they get. Exercise improves us, doing nothing does us no good at all.

Since our cells are constantly dying and new cells are being born, our psychological beliefs and attitudes are affecting these new cells and programming them. So, if we change our beliefs and attitudes, we can literally re-programme ourselves and create the body we want.

It takes effort, discipline and dedication. Most of all, it requires awareness, to be vigilant about how we think and what beliefs we are entertaining.

Anything worthwhile takes effort, discipline and dedication.

"If you always put limits on everything you do, physical or anything else, it will spread into your work and into your life. There are no limits, there are only plateaus, and you must not stay there, you must go beyond them."

Bruce Lee.

Habits

Our thoughts and beliefs become a habit. Habits can be changed. That is where the effort comes in. Most habits are unconscious. To change them we have to become conscious or aware of them. We have to have the willingness to change but who, in their right mind, wouldn't want to be willing to change if it meant delaying the effects of ageing?

Habits rarely change overnight. That is where persistence and dedication comes in.

Do you remember when you first drove your car? You got in there, behind the steering wheel and you were confronted by three pedals and you only had two feet. You had a gear stick to learn about and mirrors to check before you could move. Now you don't even think about it. Driving has become a habit.

How often have you driven home from work and could hardly remember the route you took? It has all become an automatic habit and it's easy.

All habits are like that. Good habits are empowering, but bad habits need to, and can, be changed, and that is where you apply the golden rule of Awareness, Persistence and Dedication.

Become Aware of the bad habit. Persist in eradicating it and become Dedicated to improving your own life and stretching your life span.

"Matter is Spirit moving slowly enough to be seen."

Pierre Teilhard di Chardin.

Conditioning

Most of us have rooted deep inside of us the belief 'I must age'.

Millennia ago, a famous Indian wise-man known as Shankara said, "People grow old and die because they see others grow old and die."

The late Norman Cousins said, "Belief creates Biology." Our collective expectation that the body must grow old, wear out and die, creates the biological phenomenon we refer to us ageing. If we heal that belief, we can minimise or even cancel out that expectation.

I read somewhere that scientists were studying old people in Southern Russia. These were really old people by our standards. Some of them lived to incredible ages like 140 and up to 170 years of age. Not only that, but they were fit and healthy and compos mentis.

They ate a lot of fresh fruit and vegetables and walked everywhere. Maybe that was their secret .... but could their secret really be that they saw one another live longer, healthier and fitter? Therefore creating their own collective belief? They had no visible evidence regarding ageing. They had no negative role models.

“The course of the world is not determined by physical laws. The mind has the power to affect groups of atoms and even tamper with the odds of atomic behaviour.”

Sir Arthur Stanley Eddington.
Mathematician and astrophysicist.

Self Hypnosis

In our industrialised Western world, the images we see of people in their later years of life is a sad one: Geriatrics often waiting to die. Old People's Homes populated with sedated zombies shuffling around on their Zimmer frames.

That, then, becomes our expectation and our dread.

Do not give images like that any of your attention. Be compassionate of course, and witness it, but do not see it as part of your own personal fate.

Thought is energy. Habitual thought patterns, over time, become concrete. Our thoughts and beliefs will surely manifest in our lives.

So, instead, talk to yourself. Tell yourself how young and fit and healthy and beautiful you are.

Take a deep breath. Throw back your shoulders and affirm "Every day I am becoming younger, healthier, more vital and more beautiful."

Don't just say this in an empty parrot fashion, feel it. Put some passion and feeling into what you are saying. Say it from your heart.

Breathe in this belief.

As you breathe in, visualise the Prana or Chi that is attached to each molecule of energy you are inhaling. (Prana is the Sanskrit word and Chi is the Chinese word for life energy)

See this Prana or Chi entering every cell in your body. See your cells becoming full of light and life force. Tell your body that it is now renewing itself with young, healthy, vital cells.

極

प्राण

Believe it.

Do it as often as you can. You can stop at times during your day, close your eyes and breathe in and do the above exercise of visualising the cells being filled with life force.

A very good time to do it is on waking or just as you are drifting of to sleep, your mind will be in the alpha state and will be more receptive.

You can do this sitting on a bus, train or plane. You can also take yourself off to some corner of your office for just a few minutes and do it. The more you do it the better, and you will begin to see results in a short time.

You will feel brighter, lighter and healthier. All this leads to a younger you.

"It ain't what you know that gets you into trouble. It's what you don't know for sure that just ain't so."

Mark Twain.

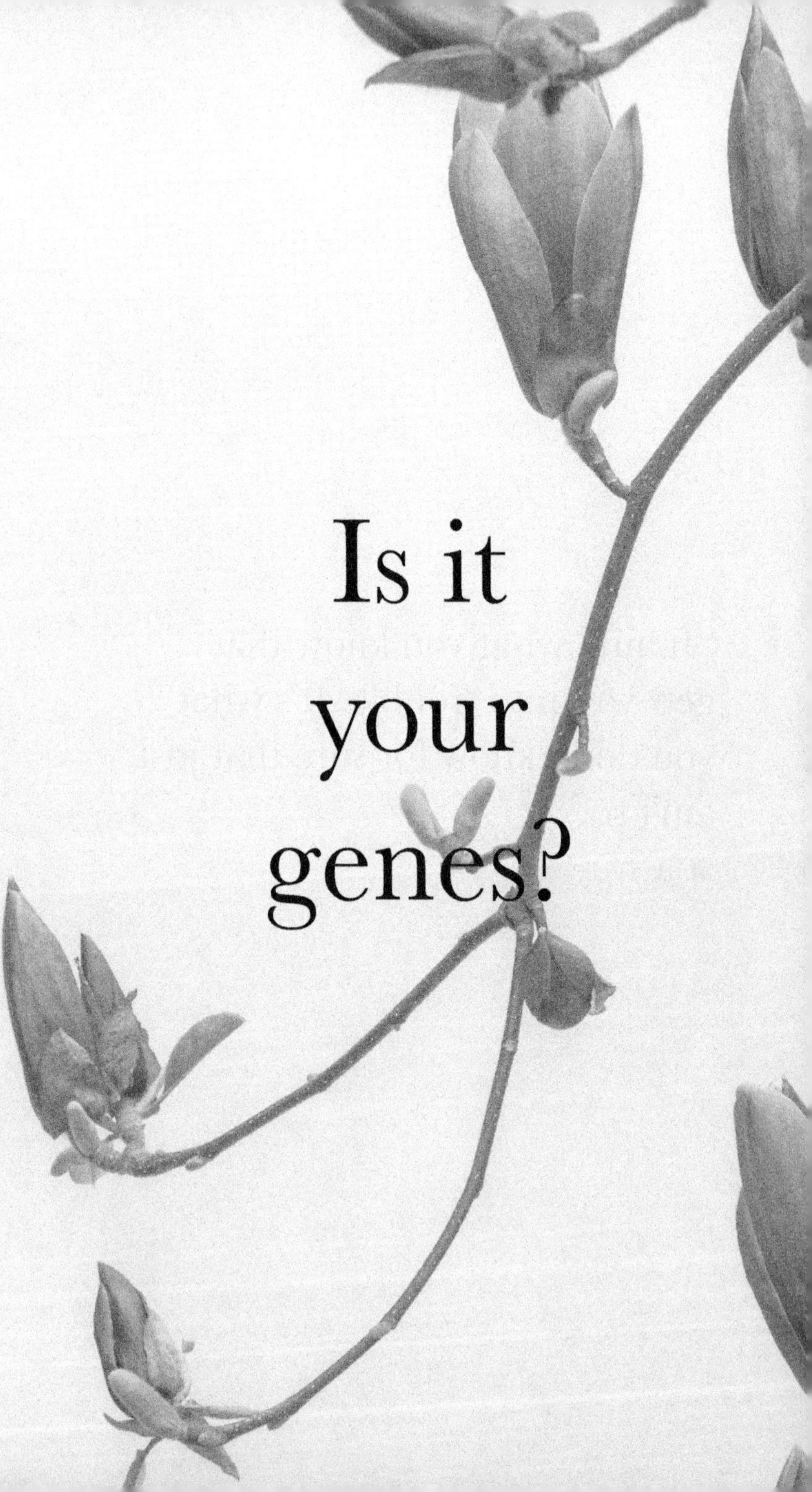

Is it your genes?

We were always told that our genes were responsible for our make-up and, consequently, our health and longevity. And, because there was no other evidence out there, we believed that idea.

There is now a whole new theory emerging called Epigenetic Theory. This theory proposes that our genes and their expression can be directly affected by environmental factors. Genes, they propose, can be turned on and off.

The Epigenetic theory (See Wikipedia) views human development as the result of an on-going bi-directional interchange between heredity and environment. Environmental influences include family dynamics, schooling, relationships, accidents we have had, traumas and diseases we have suffered and much more.

Genes do not turn themselves on and off, the environment does that. The status or combination of turned on and turned off genes is known as the epigenome—that is the overall condition or state of the cell.

In renowned cell biologist Bruce Lipton's revolutionary book on epigenetics, called 'The Biology of Belief' he describes and demonstrates how the new understanding of the link between mind and matter is profoundly affecting our understanding of how our genes work.

He shows how our genes and DNA do not control our biology, that instead DNA is controlled by signals from outside the cell, including the energetic messages emanating from our positive or negative thoughts.

To believe that our genes are the cause of our ageing is to be a victim; to believe that we have no control over our own bodies or our destiny.

To understand and to know that the scientific evidence is there to prove otherwise is empowering.

It also puts the ball back firmly in our own court—we are responsible for our own biology by our thoughts, feelings and beliefs.

What a liberating bit of information that can be.

The buck stops here! With you and me.

"Anyone who is not shocked by physics, has not understood it."

Neils Bohr. Danish Physicist.

To-Do
List ....
or
should I say,
'To BE'
list!

10

1

Change your beliefs

That is the most important action of all. I cannot emphasise this enough. Think Young. Do not entertain words which in any way suggest ageing or decay. Watch your 'Self Talk'... you know, that voice which is always nattering away in our heads.

When it is telling you negative things about yourself or your body or your ageing process, correct it. Become aware of its messages. If those messages are negative, they are not doing you any good. On the contrary, they are setting up your beliefs and are affecting your genes and your DNA. We can't shut that voice up, it is always there, but it can be trained. It can be trained to deliver positive input instead of negative. Vigilance with it pays off. The new positive way of thinking soon becomes a new habit and a new habit that will benefit you beyond measure.

"If you think you can do a thing
or think you can't do a thing,
either way you're right."

Henry Ford.

2

Keep your body moving

‘Use it or lose it’ I need not go into too much detail on the benefits of exercise in this book as there are libraries full of books on the subject. Walking is good. Dancing is better. When you dance, involve your whole body, wave your arms about, move your neck and shoulders, shake your head. Have fun!

You do not have to join a dance class, you can dance in your own living room or kitchen. Put on some lively music and get that body of yours moving. Holding weights in your hands while you dance will help to build muscle tone too.

Tai Chi is also an excellent form of exercise and increases energy and well being.

Walk whenever you can and take the stairs instead of the elevator.

"Exercise and application produce order in our affairs, health of body, cheerfulness of mind, and these make us precious to our friends."

Thomas Jefferson.

3

Eat healthily

We are what we eat. It makes perfect sense that if you want radiant health and vitality in your life, that you eat foods that have not had the life and vitality cooked or processed out of them. If you are going to boil, fry or microwave everything until it is well dead, how do you expect it to support life?

Eat foods that are as fresh as possible and still have life in them. Sprouted beans and pulses, freshly harvested, still have much life or chi in them and will give life to your life. For this, you do not need a garden, you can do your own sprouting on your kitchen window.

Raw food diets have been touted as a cure-all for many of today's diseases and I am sure that there is something in that, but how many of us , with our busy lifestyles and our commuting today, can accommodate a full raw food regime. We can, however, make sure that we have a good proportion of raw vegetables, fruits and salads in our daily diet; at least 50%

Avoid white sugar, white flour and white rice. Try a low G.I diet. There are many books on this and a plethora of information on the internet.

Drink plenty of good water. Avoid carbonated drinks. Try Green Tea for it's anti-oxidising properties.

Micro-waved foods may have their goodness destroyed. Potted plants watered with micro-waved water died while similar plants watered with non micro-waved water thrived.

4

Take Supple-ments

Since the soil on our planet is so sadly depleted, it lacks many of the elements and vital nutrients that were available even half a century ago: nutrients that are vital to our well-being. As our bodies age, they also require more of certain Vitamins, Minerals and Trace Elements.

We also need oils and fats. Essential fatty Acids are called essential, for the simple reason that they are essential. Since the introduction of Low-fat diets, obesity and its associated diseases has rocketed.

Inform yourself. After all, it is your body. See a nutritionist or a kinesiologist to determine your dietary requirements. Find out what deficiencies you suffer from and rectify the situation. Pythagoras said "Let food be thy medicine and medicine be thy food."

Buy organic, non GMO food. You will not benefit from the additives and toxins that are in many of the processed foods on the supermarket shelves today. Read the labels. Reading the labels may seem tedious to begin with, but you will soon get to know what's what, and after a while, it becomes second nature.

5

Find a role model

Find a role model,
someone older than you
who is still active, lively
and bouncing around.
If you don't know
any personally, look at
famous role models.

There are many. Michelangelo was in his 90's when he worked on the Vatican. Picasso was still a prolific painter at that age. Grandma Moses did not start painting until she was 82. She was featured on the cover of LIFE magazine at the age of 100.

Stay away from people who talk about sickness and old age. Don't play their game. You know the ones; they love to talk about their aches and pains, the medication they are on and how sick and tired they feel. Avoid words like Middle Aged, Old Age, O.A.P's, (Old age pensioners) etc. These labels have a belief associated with them that you do not need and that will not serve you well.

Play your own game. Play the game of how young you feel. 'Act as if'!

Find people who are like-minded. Look for positive people. Start your own club of Healthy Youthful Seniors. Meet up frequently with your 'club' and discuss positive things, share information on articles you have read about staying younger longer. Research on the internet and share anything good that you can bring to the club. Create a collective consciousness of friends who support these principles. Think Young. Be mentors for one another.

If we all did this, it could soon spread to the collective consciousness and radically change our world view.

Do you know the story of The Hundredth Monkey? It is an example often used to explain the collective consciousness or morphic field.

The hundredth monkey effect is a phenomenon in which a behaviour or mindset spreads rapidly from one group to all related groups once a critical number of initiates is reached.

It seems that there were some monkeys on an island, who were separated from other monkeys on other islands. One monkey discovered how to open a shell to gain food, other monkeys on that island then copied him. When the hundredth monkey on that island practiced this new skill, all the monkeys on the other islands, started to do the same. Remember they were separated by the sea and could not even see one another. The theory was used to provide evidence for the collective consciousness of the monkeys. The monkey's morphic field. We have a morphic field too.

So, as we learn to overcome some limiting behaviours, such as ageing, as soon as a critical number of us does it, we actually do it for the whole of society. What a noble and delightful thought!

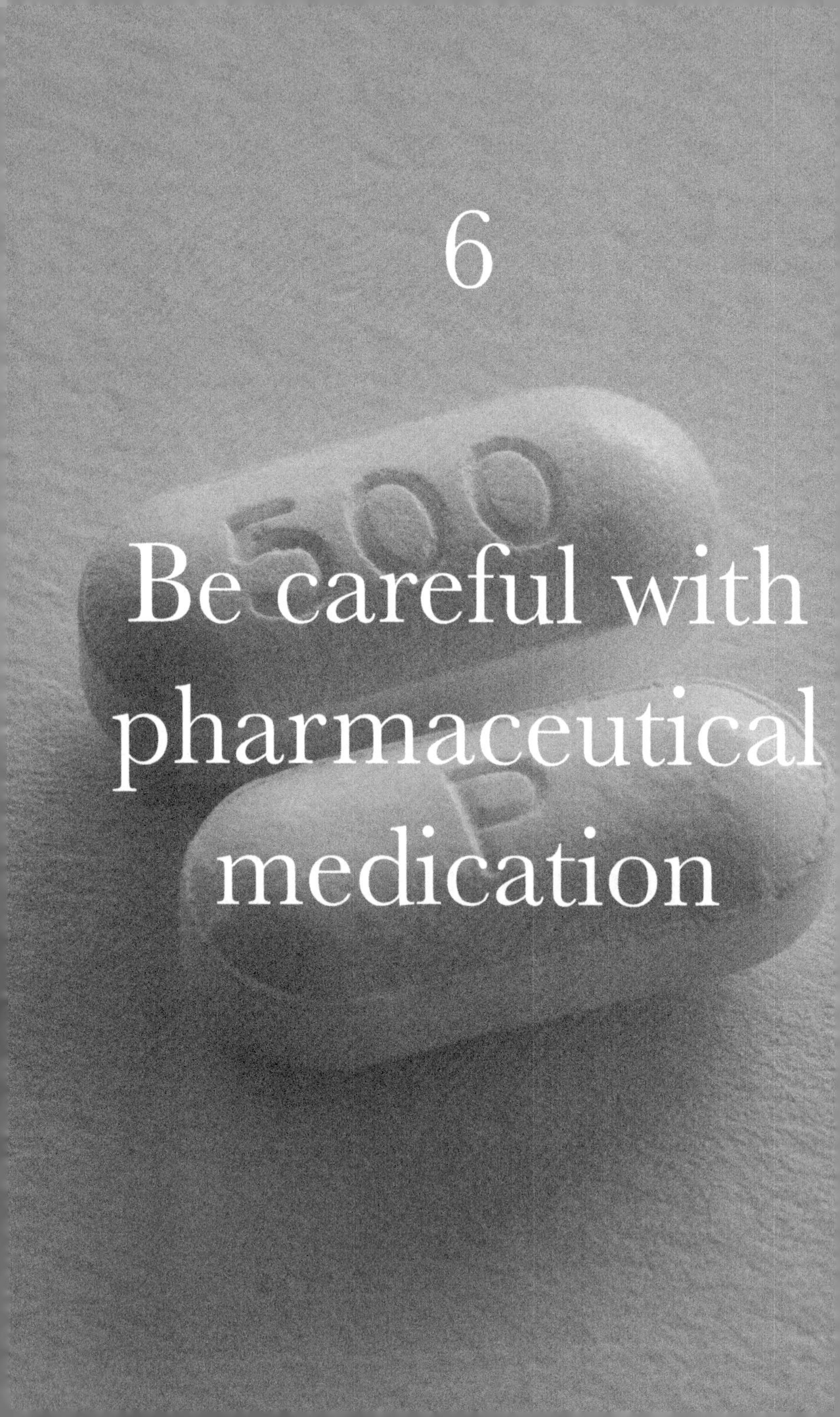

6

Be careful with pharmaceutical medication

Most drugs have side effects, then you have to be given yet another drug for the symptoms caused by the side effects, and on it goes. Older people seem to think that it is inevitable for them to have to be dependant on medication.

I am not suggesting that you ignore your doctors advice, but check and recheck. We now have access to so much information on the internet and we can learn about the effects of drugs and read other people experiences.

Instead, see what foods can be of help to your condition, find out what you may be deficient in ,check what supplements you need. There are many healthy simple remedies for most conditions.

"A person can abuse any type of prescription drug. Elderly adults commonly take 2 types of medicines that have a high potential for addiction. Growing older also slows down your body's ability to absorb and filter medicines. This means that an older adult might become addicted to or have side effects from a prescription drug at a lower dose than a younger adult."

Familydoctor.org

7

Don’t smoke

So much has been
said and written about
regarding this topic,
that anything said in
this book would be
superfluous. We all know
smoking is bad for us.

8

Cut down on alcohol consumption

Excessive alcohol consumption is, without doubt, harmful to body, mind and spirit. Monitor your own alcohol intake. Are you drinking socially or using it as medication? If it is the latter, you are entering dangerous territory. If you believe that you 'need' an alcoholic drink, you may be becoming alcohol dependant.

9

Meditate

In 1978 a UCLA physiologist called R. Keith Wallace proved that the long term practice of T.M. Meditation had a profound effect on biological ageing. He even went so far as to show that continued practice of T.M was actually reversing age!

Try your own form of meditation. Connect with your Inner Higher Power or Inner Intelligence. See the molecules of light infusing every cell of your physical body. Be aware of your breathing. Breathe in the light. This light is know in India as Prana and in China as Chi (Chi is the energy spoken of in acupuncture).

Chanting, especially chanting the different sounds through the chakras, is empowering and youthing.

As you raise your consciousness, you become more immune to decay. Your cells come and go, but your body knows how to make new ones Why not see yourself making young, new, vibrant and healthy ones and really believe it.

As you rise above the constant battle of duality; destruction and creation, you press the pause button. You slow entropy down and you move into cohesion.

"The glory of God is a human who is fully alive."

Irish Saint.

10

Be valued

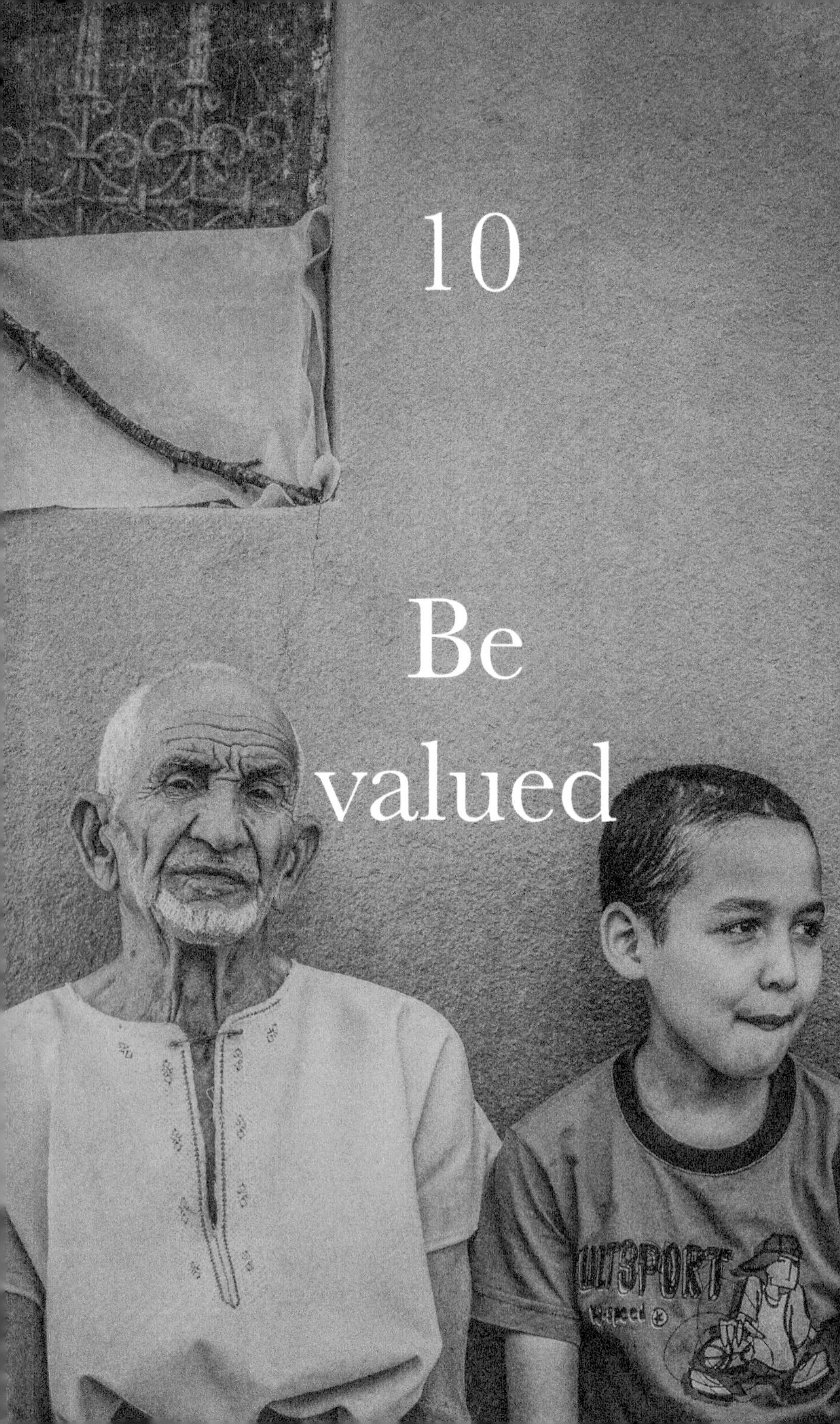

In our Western Industrialised societies older people are not valued. Why? Because in this type of society, we are conditioned to be producers; producers to feed our rampant consumerism. Consumerism is a source of great wealth for companies and corporations.

In this culture it is thought that, as people get older, they are not capable of being productive and are, instead, seen as a drain on society's resources This mind set has developed over the last few hundred years. It was not always so.

In more natural, co-operative, community based societies, older people are seen very differently. They are deferred to for the wisdom they have acquired throughout their lives. They are loved by their families and tribes or clans. They are sometimes the record keepers and are certainly seen as repositories of the communal history and wisdom.

Consequently, they are valued, and they feel valued and useful.

Neither are they pooped up to the eyeballs on every kind of drug and medication. They retain their dignity and their self-esteem. They are not marginalised, but are embraced in the bosom of their communities. There is no ageism, so they feel empowered and encouraged to live long and useful lives.

In our culture, as we grow older and become increasingly marginalised it is up to us to enlighten our fellows and to demonstrate that we are not to be easily written off.

We can educate ourselves with the facts and not the conventional thinking regarding ageing. We can explore the scientific breakthroughs.

We can push the boundaries. We can be the pioneers of a New Old Age Revolution!

"Before you become elderly; learn how to care, respect and love elder-ones since you will be that one thereupon and ultimately."

Ehsan Sehgal.

Wise Ones.
Shift the
paradigm.

Change your beliefs about ageing. As you do it for yourself, you do it for all. As I explained previously in the reference to The Hundredth Monkey Syndrome, as one changes, all are affected. We are all connected. You can be the inspiration for those around you.

Share your findings as you do your research. Share your ideas. Inspire your fellows and Be the change.

Accept nothing less than the very best; from life, from your body, from your friends and family and from your community.

Get out there and Do something with your life. It is never too late to start something new.

Wouldn't it be great if the
older people grouped together
to lobby for better conditions
in villages, towns and cities.
Older people could be a force
for wisdom and guidance today
as they were in ancient more
civilised times.

If you are still young and you think these ideas don't apply to you. Be aware, they will one day, and if you apply some of the ideas I have shared with you in this book, you can defer the age process indefinitely. It all depends on how much you want it, and who wouldn't want it?

"The secret of genius is to carry the spirit of the child into old age, which means never losing your enthusiasm."

Aldous Huxley.

Recommended Reading

'The Spontaneous Healing of Belief'

By Gregg Braden.
www.greggbraden.com

'Ageless Body, Timeless Mind'

By Deepak Chopra, M.D.

'The Biology of Belief'

By Bruce Lipton, Ph.D.

'Age Power'

By Leslie Kenton.

‘Breaking the Habit of Being Yourself’

By Dr. Joe Dispenza.

‘The Science of Mind’

By Ernest Holmes.

Other books by Anne Hassett

'Reading Your Child's Hand'

Discover your child's talents and abilities and help him/her to develop their potential in life.

'Discover the Innate Potential of Children'

Co-written with Marianne Volonte. The knowledge of the information given in the fingerprints and hands of children is a must for all parents and other caregivers such as teachers, therapists and doctors. Fingerprints and hand patterns allow access to the complete picture: positive and critical character traits as well as potential and challenges. A toll which cannot be faked, altered or controlled.

'The Power of saying F*** it'

A very spiritual book with a naughty title! It tells you how to move from operating from Ego and to work instead from Higher Self.

'Angel Whispers'

Short inspiring messages channelled from the Angels by Acushla (Anne Hassett)

‘Just for The Craic’

A funny novel about Irish building workers in Swindon.

All of these books are available from Amazon.

I also offer one-to-one sessions.

See the website www.quantumrecoding.com

About Anne

Anne Hassett, who has been psychic since childhood, chose the name Acushla to honour her Celtic origins and to have a name in keeping with her mission in life, which is to heal.

The word Acushla in Gaelic means 'Pulse' (of the heart) or 'love' in the sense of compassion.

Clients come from all over the country, and from parts of Europe, to see her in Bath, where she has been based for thirty one years. She travels to several countries in Europe and has worked in America, Australia, New Zealand, The

Middle East, and Far East. For twenty three years Acushla has worked several times a year in Hong Kong, where she has a large and loyal following. She has featured on TV and radio, and in many international newspapers and magazines. She counts many celebrities and media stars among her clientele..

Acushla communicates with angels all the time and sees them around her clients when she is doing psychic readings. She is known for her no-nonsense approach in helping her clients with their problems and is well known for the accuracy of her insights. Her approach is a loving one and even if she sees something challenging or negative in a reading she will always give some guidance on how to overcome the problem and will suggests ways to create an alternative and more satisfying reality.

Acushla works closely with her main guide, a very ancient Chinese sage called Master Ho. She has strong connections with Jesus, Saint Germain, Mary Magdalen and Kwan Yin who assist her in her psychic and her healing work.

Printed in Great Britain
by Amazon

41977723R00098